Understanding the Impact of Divorce on Christian Families

Pastoral and Theological Insights

Reverend Walter Orinda

Copyright

Book formatting and editing: Dr Jacqueline N Samuels

https://tinyurl.com/AuthorJNSamuels

Amazon Paperback ISBN: **9798865471622**

Connect on YouTube: **@newlifedestinybaptistchurch1**

Contents

Dedication

This book is dedicated to every married couple, intending couple, and every individual who has experienced marital challenges. Your unique life is a testament of God's healing and restorative grace. As you remain closely linked to the Vine, may God's Presence daily guide your relationship. Allow Him to nurture and direct your footsteps and purpose.

Acknowledgements

While it is not possible to mention every person who has contributed towards this book's reality, it is important to acknowledge several individuals who have impacted this journey:

Thank You faithful Holy Spirit. Your constant Presence and Guidance helped to birth this book.

I am deeply grateful to Pastor Lillian Orinda, my dear wife and co-worker in the ministry for constantly encouraging me and releasing me to complete the research for this work.

Sincere thanks to my supervisor, Dr Claire Watkins (University of Roehampton UK) for sharing your professional and spiritual expertise throughout my master's studies.

Sincere gratitude to Apostle Robert Ntefon for your insightful Foreword and encouragement on a topic close to your heart.

This book would not have been published without the expert mentoring, guidance and encouragement by my book editor, publisher and cover designer, Dr Jacqueline N Samuels. Thank you for your commitment to seeing this project through.

To everyone who has contributed to the case studies, thank you.

To all who have shared insightful suggestions on the topic of marriage, divorce and support for affected parties, I appreciate your time and candid honesty.

May the LORD Almighty bless you all.

Reverend Walter Orinda

Connect on YouTube: **@newlifedestinybaptistchurch1**

Many are the afflictions of the righteous,
But the Lord delivers him out of them all.
(Psalm 34:19)

Foreword

Marriage is one of life's most profound commitments, binding two souls together as one. Yet when marriages fail, the resultant divorce brings deep wounds that impact entire families. In this important book, Reverend Walter Orinda examines the ripple effects of divorce through the lens of Christian theology.

With care and wisdom, Reverend Orinda explores how the major branches of Christianity have wrestled with the reality of divorce over the centuries. Studying these differing viewpoints, it becomes clear there are no easy answers. Each tradition grapples in its own way with upholding the sanctity of marriage while extending grace to those whose marriages have broken apart.

As Reverend Orinda insightfully notes, the Church is called to walk alongside hurting families with mercy, not judgment. Our role is not to condemn but to care – offering the balm of God's love to all who suffer from divorce's scars. Wise pastoral care can help guide people through the storm, stirring hope that they may yet live abundant lives.

Reverend Orinda has provided a thoughtful guidebook for responding to divorce's thorny issues. This book will assist clergy and congregations in ministering with compassion to those hurting from divorce while honouring the holy union of marriage.

I'm reminded of something I once heard that *problems are simply opportunities dressed in work clothes*. Divorce presents challenges, yes, but also openings to show God's auspicious love. My hope is this book will spark fresh understanding, so the Church can bring comfort and redemption to lives impacted by divorce.

With care and clarity, Reverend Orinda has shone an edifying light on a painful subject. May all who read it be uplifted in spirit.

Apostle Robert Ntefon

Marriage Coaches Trainer & Founder:

http://sozobibleschool.com

Endorsements

To many, 'divorce' is a simple word to define, and the process to effect it is just as simple.

In this book, Rev. Walter Orinda interrogates the complexities of the impact of divorce through a comparative analysis of three Christian perspectives. By so-doing, he not only contributes to a much-needed voice in Pastoral theology on divorce, but also avails a tool through which those confronted with the challenges of divorce and its aftermath may find solace and encouragement.

For those whose marriage still stands, the book provides scriptural and theological insights that can be tapped to solidify their union. For those involved in Christian ministry, this book will be a valuable resource in spiritual counselling. It is a book for all, and I highly recommend it.

Reverend Joel Mwirigi

Founder and Senior Pastor:

https://www.jesuschristtheministry.org.uk/

The institute of marriage is the only test where people are given a certificate before taking the exam. As a result, many couples who feel they have failed the 'exam' often opt to divorce as a way out, leaving stranded children and broken hearts in their wake. While there are many factors that lead to marriage breakup, unresolved issues affecting dependents are often ignored.

What is the spiritual and emotional significance of divorce upon the affected families? Sometimes this starts a spiral of similar breakups that children and siblings may follow without considering the effects on the wider community.

The author has highlighted various religious views on divorce and the disparities that further complicate the affected couples spiritual growth and acceptance to aid the healing process.

Before the early twenty-first century, many couples would never speak about divorce as a normal occurrence. Further, our parents followed the principles of marriage, opting to remain and work it out despite encountering numerous challenges along the way. Many in my age group were taught to adjust and make it work for the sake of the children and to maintain the family's good name.

This book is an eye-opener, pertinent for present-day new and seasoned couples, believers and non-believers.

Thank you, Reverend Orinda, for opening this timely topic on **_Understanding the Impact of Divorce on Christian Families._** The extensive research provides welcome avenues for spiritual and emotional healing after divorce and guidance for pastoral counselling opportunities.

Pastor Lillian Orinda

Wife, mother, pastor, author

Co-Pastor at New Life Destiny Baptist Church

Website: https://newlifedbc.org/

YouTube: @newlifedestinybaptistchurch1

In the compassionate ministry of Reverend Walter Orinda, w find a shepherd whose heart resonates with the joys an struggles of the Christian family. With years of pastora experience and a deep well of wisdom, Rev. Walter unveils th poignant realities faced by Christian families navigating th profound challenges of divorce.

Understanding the Impact of Divorce on Christian Families

In this insightful work, Rev. Walter delves into the sacre tapestry of God's purpose for marriage, unraveling the thread that bind hearts in covenant. From the very outset, readers ar invited to embark on a journey of understanding, where th complexities of marital dissolution are met with biblical truth grace, and an unwavering commitment to the redemptive powe of Christ.

With a firm foundation in Scripture, Rev. Walter paints a vivi picture of God's original intent for marriage—a divine unio grounded in love, mutual support, and the reflection of Hi covenant with His people.

Beyond the surface, Rev. Walter examines the intrica structures that shape Christian families. His exploratio encompasses the roles, responsibilities, and sacred bonds tha form the backbone of these unions.

Throughout the book, a wealth of practical insights awaits the reader. From navigating the emotional terrain of divorce to rebuilding lives with faith at the center, Pastor Walter addresses the multifaceted aspects of this challenging journey.

In these pages, Rev. Walter's words emerge as a balm for wounded hearts, offering not just understanding but a path toward healing and restoration. This book is not a mere exploration of a difficult subject; it is a testament to Rev. Walter's heart for families—a heart that beats in rhythm with the compassionate love of the Savior.

As you turn the pages of ***Understanding the Impact of Divorce on Christian Families***, may you find a guiding light, a source of comfort, and a renewed sense of God's redemptive power amid life's storms.

Blessings,

Rev. Peter Kamau

Higher Heights Church

https://www.facebook.com/HigherHeightsChurchUK/

And above all things have fervent love for one another,
for "love will cover a multitude of sins."
(1 Peter 4:8)

Introduction

The issue of divorce against the background of Christian doctrine through the ages is an often-traumatic phenomenon.

We will begin by reflecting on the origin of marriage as God ordained it in Genesis chapter 2 and examine the various repercussions of breakdown of this great institution.

We will then employ a comparative approach to examine three mainstream perspectives namely the Roman Catholic Church's view, the Liberal Church's view and the Evangelical Church's view.

The scriptural basis for each perspective is first considered followed by an account of key historical traditions that have influenced each of these positions. We will explore the impact of each perspective on Christian families. The wide range of evidence used includes Old and New Testament scriptures, historic commentaries and official statements of faith, academic books and articles, as well as modern websites and journalistic sources. We will address three key questions:

Are the significant differences in theological interpretation and pastoral practice likely to remain across different Christian denominations?

Is there a general shift towards a greater tolerance of divorce?

How can we focus on dealing compassionately with its aftermath within the different Church branches?

Besides reflecting on the theological and pastoral roles and impact we aim to suggest useful recommendations for those charged with pastoral responsibility.

Chapter ONE: God's Purpose for Marriage

The book of Genesis 2:18-24 records God's Divine purpose and plan for marriage.

> *And the Lord God said, **"It is not good that man should be alone; I will make him a helper comparable to him."** Out of the ground the Lord God formed every beast of the field and every bird of the air, and brought them to Adam to see what he would call them. And whatever Adam called each living creature, that was its name. So Adam gave names to all cattle, to the birds of the air, and to every beast of the field. But for Adam there was not found a helper comparable to him. **And the Lord God caused a deep sleep to fall on Adam, and he slept; and He took one of his ribs, and closed up the flesh in its place.** Then the rib which the Lord God had taken from man He made into a woman, and He brought her to the man.*

And Adam said: "This is now bone of my bones and flesh of my flesh; she shall be called Woman, because she was taken out of Man." **Therefore a man shall leave his father and mother and be joined to his wife, and they shall become one flesh.** (Emphasis mine)

God created the heavens, earth and all living things and calle it good. However, after creating man in His Own image an likeness (Gen. 1:26), God said it was not good for man to b alone and created a helpmate (Gen. 2:18). Adam named h helpmate "*Woman*" because she came from his rib. Throug the act of human creation in male and female form God create and blessed the marriage institution (Gen. 1:27-28):

So God created man in His own image; in the image of God He created him; male and female He created them. Then God blessed them, *and God said to them, "Be fruitful and multiply; fill the earth and subdue it; have dominion over the fish of the sea, over the birds of the air, and over every living thing that moves on the earth."* (Emphasis mine)

The marriage institution is designed to empower male and female couples to co-exist in a holy and honourable union that pleases God.

What happens when two people are ill suited, or fall out of love?

What are the repercussions when married couples are hostile to one another or lose respect for the marriage union?

Such challenges sometimes lead to divorce which in turn opens new doors of pain, bitterness, blame, broken homes and more.

The Holy Bible repeatedly calls on individuals including couples to love one another, forgive one another and bear with one another in love.

Ephesians 5:25-33 instructs husbands and wives on how to relate to one another within the marriage covenant.

Husbands, love your wives, just as Christ also loved the church and gave Himself for her, that He might sanctify and cleanse her with the washing of water by the word, that He might present her to Himself a glorious church, not having spot or wrinkle or any such thing, but that she should be holy and without blemish.

So husbands ought to love their own wives as their own bodies; he who loves his wife loves himself. For no one ever hated his own flesh, but nourishes and cherishes it, just as the Lord does the church.

For we are members of His body, of His flesh and of His bones. *"For this reason a man shall leave his father and mother and be joined to his wife, and the two shall become one flesh."*

This is a great mystery, but I speak concerning Christ and the church. Nevertheless let each one of you in particular so love his own wife as himself, and let the wife see that she respects her husband.

(Ephesians 5:25-33)

What about couples who don't know the Scriptures? How do they cope with unforeseen trials?

They may seek guidance and counselling from various religious or secular institutions. When all doors of reconciliation fail, whatever the couples' religious affiliation, the only alternative left is to end the marriage. Therein lies the challenge as many couples leave behind wounded children, broken hearts and countless unresolved issues in their wake.

If the foundations are destroyed, what can the righteous do? (Ps. 11:3)

What options are in place for Christian couples who end up in a broken relationship? In the following pages we will address the marriage structure and impact of divorce among Christian families.

Chapter TWO: Marriage Structures

All human societies have their own deeply embedded traditions which serve to give structure to relationships and keep everyday life running smoothly. The many relationships depicted in the Bible also reflect this core structure, since God stands in a **parent** relationship to His people, and Christ stands in the relationship of **groom** to the Church's role of **bride** (Balswick and Balswick).

The nuclear family is based on a monogamous couple staying together for life and bringing up any children together. This core unit underpins Christian family life and mirrors this Divine model. This family structure is exemplified many times in the Bible and ratified by all Christian churches as the ideal for most Christians.

It can be as small as a single couple and may also include grandparents and other close relatives or dependents as Moxnes reflects in *What is family? Problems in constructing early Christian families*.

Other options include celibacy, taking up service in a religious order, or entering the priesthood within the Roman Catholic church. Since New Testament times to the present-day, marriage and founding a family have been presented as the norm for most Christians. These usually involve a ceremonial rite performed by the relevant local church leader.

Marriage is also ratified in most cultures by legal structures, emphasising its importance in terms of allocating formal responsibility for children, property and wealth or possessions. As an institution, marriage has provided security and stability for countless millions of people, and it is designed to provide a crucial nurturing environment for children and young people. They are taught moral and religious values as well as the skills and knowledge required for adult life.

Sometimes married life does not run smoothly for couples as evidenced in modern Western societies where more and more marriages are breaking down. Feminist scholar Weitzmann, in *The Divorce Revolution* argues that this contributes to serious societal problems such as domestic violence, child neglect and emotional distress which affect women more than men.

Divorce rates have been rising steadily in Western countries since the mid-1960s. At the same time the proportion of people who live together without the formal ratification of a civil or religious marriage rite has been on the rise as Demo and Acock note in *The Impact of Divorce upon Children*.

Changing values in society have resulted in differing meaning of marriage over time. New problems have also arisen out the greater prevalence of divorce in recent decades, as Ama notes in *Research on Divorce: Continuing Trends and Ne Developments*.

This discussion examines one issue that stems out of these wide-ranging social trends namely the impact divorce has c Christian families including husbands and wives who divorc the children of divorcing parents, and the rest of the nucle family including grandparents and other close relatives.

Chapter THREE: Scope of the Study

Since there are many different perspectives on the phenomenon of divorce even within Church communities, it is not possible to reflect every view in this book. We will therefore not look at the causes of divorce or the wider impact of divorce upon society. Our scope will focus on examining the impact of divorce on Christian families.

In *Marriage and the Family: A Christian Perspective,* Grunlan argues that the rising divorce rates among Christians is also becoming a crisis of parenthood. Widespread scholarly evidence reveals negative short term and longer-term impacts of divorce on families in general alongside psychological or developmental difficulties and lower educational outcomes for children of divorced parents.

Further examples are found in Amato and Keith, in *Parental Divorce and the Well-Being of Children: A Meta-Analysis*; Amato in *The consequences of divorce for adults and children*; Root, in *The Children of Divorce: The Loss of Family as the Loss of Being*).

These negative impacts can also arise from related factors such as parental absence, family conflict and economic disadvantage.

The economic impact of divorce is much worse for women than for men, affecting some social and ethnic groups more than others. In their article *The Future of Children*, Teachman and Paasch note the need for careful examination of institutional policies which are designed to respond to divorce.

The starting point for this discussion is the general background of rising rates of divorce in Western societies and the presence of demonstrably negative impacts of divorce upon families, which are particularly devastating to children. For further evidence on the negative impact of divorce see Fagan, P. F. and Churchill, A., *The Effects of Divorce on Children: Research Synthesis.*

The focus here, however, is on the sub-set of families who are part of a Christian church community alongside the theological and spiritual dimensions of divorce. Many Christians experience divorce themselves, or in their immediate family group, and this can have quite severe consequences in terms of their Christian faith, alongside their position and standing within the Church community.

Why this particular focus?

Although there is a rather large literature on the issue of divorce in pastoral theology textbooks and articles, much of it is concerned with the laudable aim of preventing divorce from occurring through counselling and other support before and during marriage.

However, there is considerably less literature available on the impact of divorce on the Christian families and the pastoral challenges of dealing with this situation once it has happened.

Furthermore, the global Christian Church has developed different theological positions and official policies on the issue of divorce, following the diverging traditions of the various mainstream denominations. This has led to some uncertainty about the underpinning theology that guides Christian beliefs on this issue which might be used to inform pastoral responses.

There appears to be a lack of clarity on the theological basis for different positions, the need for reform, and the impact of different policies on families who are directly affected by divorce.

Regardless of their Christian or secular perspective, most social workers recognize that social support is a crucial factor both in reinforcing marital stability and helping people who are experiencing difficulties in their marriage to cope. (Refer to Amato, Booth, Johnson and Rogers, *Alone Together: How Marriage in America is Changing,* p. 181).

The church's role as a social institution is therefore a crucial factor for Christian families as they navigate the difficult territory that comes with divorce and its aftermath.

Aims of the Study

How Christian pastors can and should respond to the tension between the biblical ideal of lifelong marriage with the reality of divorce in the modern world is something that requires further insight. Current knowledge and practice differ widely between different denominations, and often also between different congregations within the same denominations. This variation causes difficulty for many Christians and pastoral care professionals alike.

This book seeks first to critically examine a range of mainstream Christian responses to divorce. Secondly, it aims to explore the impact of that divorce. Finally, we offer recommendations for pastoral support enhanced by our findings in the pursuit of the initial two aims.

Research Questions

The two main research questions this discussion seeks to answer are:

1) How have different branches of the Christian Church responded to the issue of divorce?

2) What impact does divorce itself and these responses have on Christian family members at the present time?

The first of these questions needs to be approached from multiple perspectives. This will help to identify the range of different responses that have been suggested at different times in different parts of the world, following different denominational directions.

There are theological and practical dimensions to the various responses. It is also important to note that there is bound to be some distance between official church doctrine and the actual practices that take place within each community. When it comes to assessing the impact of current responses, it is necessary to seek out first-hand testimonies from pastors and congregations and to consider academic studies on contemporary divorce that include religious faith as a factor for analysis.

Chapter FOUR: Method and Structure

Given the contentious nature of divorce within the globa Christian Church, it is unlikely that a single, clear answer ca be given to any of the research questions outlined in th previous section. We expect a range of answers will be found each reflecting different aspects of the problem alongsid different historical and traditional ways of approaching pastora work in cases of divorce. The aim here is not to argue for c against any denomination's teachings or policies, but rather t explore and understand the reasons that lie behind differer positions and to assess their impact on Christian families.

The two-fold structure of this work consists of the academic pa of this study which has two introductory chapters followed b three main case study chapters. A separate section c theological and pastoral reflection is provided thereafter whic includes some personal views on the different perspectives tha were presented in the main body of the research.

Finally, some conclusions and a set of recommendations fc pastoral care professionals are offered in the final chapter.

The final chapter also makes some suggestions on how best to counsel and support Christian families experiencing divorce, and how to avoid some of the negative impacts and needlessly painful experiences that have been identified in the earlier chapters.

Comparative Method

A comparative method is selected for this investigation because it allows these multiple cases to stand alongside each other, showing the range of issues that have arisen, and the solutions that have been found in each case. This method is indispensable to scholars of religion because it highlights both the particularities of individual religions and the universals. This in turn is invaluable in the quest for knowledge and deeper understanding, as Segal *In Defense of the Comparative Method* p. 339 notes.

The three major Christian perspectives examined are:

i) The Roman Catholic perspective, as taught by the Vatican and the official documents of that Church.

ii) The broadly liberal, reformed perspective, which includes the Church of England, Methodist churches, and many others, which usually pursue a more open and flexible interpretation of Scripture.

iii) Thirdly, the Evangelical perspective, which includes Presbyterian, Baptist, and Pentecostal perspectives, which often rest on a rather more literal interpretation of Scripture.

It is worth recognizing from the onset that all three positions can co-exist within each of the large denominations, and it is often difficult to draw clear boundaries between Roman Catholic, Liberal and Evangelical groups.

Indeed, some ecumenical groups may combine all three perspectives, seeking unity in diversity which makes it very difficult to draw hard and fast conclusions about any specific congregation at any given time. However, a broad sketch of each position is a realistic goal as this study reveals.

Critical Literature Review

The approach chosen here is to trace the concept of divorce through a critical literature review. Relevant statements from key theologians from each branch are identified and examined, including commentaries on Scriptural sources. Comments on and reactions to significant events in history that have bearing on this subject are also noted.

The current official position of each branch is explained, with reference to contemporary guidance given by major denominations. Where necessary, regional and cultural variation is also mentioned, as evidence of the range of positions on divorce that have been developed across the world.

Selection and Analysis of Website Evidence

Critical literature review is very useful for establishing the current official position on divorce in various Church setups and explaining why different conclusions were reached by different groups and denominations. It also helps to identify and understand the major theological issues raised.

However, it is not very helpful when it comes to gauging the impact of divorce on Christian families. Therefore, a range of secular academic sources are reviewed to illuminate more on this topical focus, mainly sociological and psychological studies, and a few websites and journalistic sources.

First-hand accounts from pastors, divorcing or divorced couples and their families provide additional relevant evidence on how the policies and practices of the various churches are working out for families.

This evidence provides insights into the good and bad outcomes that arise for Christian families who experience divorce, and the effect of individuals' beliefs, the teachings o their priest or pastor, and the reactions of the Christian anc secular community.

Websites were selected using standard searches in Google such as 'divorce + church' and 'divorce + Christian'. Links to newspapers, magazines, blogs and support group sites were also identified using a snowball method of following links anc posts that were provided with each main site. Several specialis websites giving guidance and advice to pastoral care professionals and to Christian families about divorce were also included.

Since there is no way of telling how far this sample is representative of all Christian communities and Christian families experiencing divorce and its aftermath, no generalizations can be made in the findings. However, this first hand data can give some very useful and up-to-date information on the actual impact on some families today, as well as an barriers or aids to Christian priests and pastors in supporting such families.

Scope and Limitations

The scope of this study is deliberately broad. It seeks to present an overview of divorce and its impact on Christian families across all the major denominations. This has the advantage of avoiding narrow interpretations. On the other hand, such a broad focus means that it is impossible, for reasons of space, to go into the topic very deeply.

This broad scope also means that the conclusions reached at the end must be couched in broad terms, allowing for the possibility that more than one solution to the issues raised can be valid and effective. Contextual factors and historical or traditional influences will necessarily reduce the options available to different Christian communities, and this is accepted as a necessary limitation for this study.

Chapter FIVE: Roman Catholic Perspective

Scriptural Basis

The institution of marriage as a permanent, legally bindin commitment is made clear in the book of Genesis: *For th reason a man will leave his father and mother and be united t his wife, and the two will become one flesh.* (Gen. 2:24.)

Throughout the Old Testament there is plenty of evidence tha divorce was permitted among the Jewish people according t Jewish law, so long as the divorcing husband gave the divorce wife a certificate to that effect, thereby legitimising her status s that she could remarry.

This situation lies behind the instruction in Deuteronomy 24:1- regarding marriage (permitted), divorce (permitted) an remarriage to the same woman after a second divorce widowhood (not permitted). The passage states:

If a man marries a woman who becomes displeasing to him because he finds something indecent about her, and he writes her a certificate of divorce, gives it to her and sends her from his house, and if after she leaves his house she becomes the wife of another man, and her second husband dislikes her and writes her a certificate of divorce, gives it to her and sends her from his house, or if he dies, then her first husband, who divorced her, is not allowed to marry her again after she has been defiled. That would be detestable in the eyes of the Lord. Do not bring sin upon the land the Lord your God is giving you as an inheritance.

The grounds for divorce are somewhat vaguely referred to in terms of "indecency".

The book of Malachi, which was written much later in Jewish history, contains an equally cryptic reference to divorce. Jones notes that the original Septuagint version of Mal. 2:16 is preserved in two different variants. This has led to two varying translations namely, "If you hate, divorce!" - an imperative which may, or may not, be ironic - and "If hating you divorce" — referring to divorce out of hatred (see Jones in *A Note on the LXX of Malachi 2:16, Journal of Biblical Literature*, p. 683).

This same text was also interpreted in two different ways by the early Patristic commentators since Theodore of Mopsuetia and Theodoret of Cyrrhus assumed the first version and Cyril of Alexandria and Jerome the second. (Ibid., pp. 683-684.)

The online version of New International Version translates Mal. 2:16 as *"The man who hates and divorces his wife," says the Lord, the God of Israel, "does violence to the one he should protect," says the Lord Almighty."* It also offers an alternative reading *"I hate divorce," says the Lord, the God of Israel, "because the man who divorces his wife covers his garment with violence."*

The latter interpretation has been used to justify an absolute prohibition of divorce, and doubtless explains the durability of the conservative position still visible in the Roman Catholic Church today. In the New Testament there is a similar disapproval for divorce in the teachings of Jesus who said: *"I tell you that anyone who divorces his wife, except for sexual immorality, and marries another woman commits adultery."* (Mt. 19:9)

Historical Tradition

The early Church's position was rather more liberal on the issue of divorce than the contemporary Catholic Church.

Fiorenza reports that Patristic commentators including Origen, Basil, Ambrosiaster and Augustine all refer to the early church's practice of allowing both divorce on the grounds of adultery and marriage thereafter. (See Fiorenza, "Marriage" in *Systematic Theology: Roman Catholic Perspectives.* p. 616.)

However, Augustine's argument that marriage was a sacrament, followed by the efforts of Thomas Aquinas to organise the rules on marriage and divorce into Canon Law had the effect of consolidating a strict position on divorce. The argument used by Thomas Aquinas rests on the parallel between man's union with his wife and Christ's union with the Church, both of which are assumed to be ordained by God and indissoluble even in the context of one party's sinful nature and behaviour. (Ibid., pp. 617-618.)

In 1563 the Council of Trent resisted the leniency of the reformers and reaffirmed the Catholic prohibitions on divorce and remarriage. The decision set in stone the sacramental character of marriage, thereby implying that no divorce is possible since that union is for life. *(Source: The Canons and Decrees of the Sacred and Oecumenical Council of Trent* in Waterworth: http://history.hanover.edu/texts/trent.html)

Current Doctrine

There has been little change in recent years in the strong position of the Roman Catholic Church against divorce. The Roman Catholic Catechism declares that *"Divorce is a grave offense against the natural law"* ... [and] does injury to the covenant of salvation, of which sacramental marriage is a sign' (Source: *Catechism of the Catholic Church.* Second edition.)

Marriage is regarded as a permanent communion between two persons but those who wish to separate from their spouse may request an annulment through a lengthy and often difficult application process. (Source: Onedera, *The Role of Religion in Marriage and Family Counseling,* pp. 46-47.)

In recent years there has been a relaxation of the factors that can be taken as grounds for annulment to include "lack of understanding, lack of partnership and conjugal love psychological immaturity, psychopathic and schizophrenic personality and several other reasons". (Fiorenza, p. 616.)

Divorce has been recognized as a disputed issue within the Church, one that theologians need to work on to respond to the increasing tensions it causes. (A full rehearsal of the disputed points is provided by Lawlor, *Marriage and the Catholic Church Disputed Questions*).

More recently there are evident signs that the Roman Catholic Church is beginning to review its policy on divorce, with some journalists reporting a slight shift towards more lenient rulings following the emphasis on mercy in the papacy of Pope Francis. (See Goodstein and Povoledo, *Amid Splits, Catholic Bishops Crack Open Door on Divorce.*)

Pope Francis stated,

> *"The Eucharist, although it is the fullness of sacramental life, is not a prize for the perfect but a powerful medicine and nourishment for the weak. These convictions have pastoral consequences that we are called to consider with prudence and boldness."*

(Source: Pope Francis, cited in Scalia, *Pope Francis's quiet campaign to rethink divorce in the Catholic Church*. The Guardian.)

This does indeed appear to embrace a more tolerant attitude towards divorce but as Church history has shown, change can be very slow to take effect.

Impact on Families

The prohibition on divorce within the Roman Catholic Churc combined with social forces that lead to marriage breakdown the modern world has had a major impact on those affecte Divorced people often feel doubly rejected, first by the spous who is no longer with them, and secondly by the church whic does not allow them to pursue a new relationship and remain fellowship with other Christians.

According to Duffy "*many people are blindsided by divorce, . doubt, shame and fear of being judged are constant themes th keep them away from parish activities*". (Source: Duffy, *7 wa Parish Leaders Can Better Serve Divorced Catholics*.)

Since the Church does not always grant annulments, the on option recommended in such a situation is lifelong chastit even when the decision to separate was taken by the spous or when the separation was caused by infidelity or some oth serious failing on the spouse's part. This creates obviou difficulties for divorced couples within the Roman Cathol community.

Researchers have also tracked some movement in ordina believers' views, noting that *the moral authority of the church . family matters may have declined in recent years with Catholic becoming less distinct*. (Source: Thornton, *Changing Attitude toward Separation and Divorce: Causes and Consequences*, 858.)

H. Wayne House explains this trend in a study which includes contributions from many different authors, each with their own perspective on the issue of divorce. (Source: House, *Divorce and Remarriage: Four Christian Views.*)

One of the most serious consequences of the Roman Catholic position on divorce using the annulment process is that it deems the children of any such marriage to be in effect illegitimate. Another serious consequence is that due to the challenges couples have in navigating the complex and intrusive annulment process, many opt instead to use the secular and legal divorce processes to end a marriage.

Roman Catholics who do this however, and especially those who start a new relationship or remarry thereafter, are not permitted to take part in the Holy Eucharist. They are effectively excluded from full community access with the rest of the Church. There has been official recognition of the pain that this formal exclusion brings to divorced parties who have remarried outside the Church procedures as evidenced in this message from the Synod of Bishops in 2005 which should be read in full to understand the implications it conveys:

> *"We know the sadness of those who do not have access to sacramental communion because of their family situations that do not conform to the commandment of the Lord (see Mt. 19:3-9).*

Some divorced and remarried people sadly accept their inability to take sacramental communion and they make an offering of it to God. Others are not able to understand this restriction, and live with an internal frustration. We reaffirm that, while we do not endorse their choice (cf. CCC.2384), they are not excluded from the life of the Church. We ask that they participate in Sunday Mass and devote themselves assiduously to listening to the Word of God so that it might nourish their life of faith, of love and of conversion. We wish to tell them how close we are to them in prayer and pastoral concern. Together, let us ask the Lord to obey his will faithfully". (Source: *Message of the XI Ordinary General Assembly of the Synod of Bishops.* para. 15.)

This very strict ruling means divorce and remarriage amount to permanent excommunication. The Roman Catholic Church accepts the reality of marriage breakdown, but does not permit any concessions, including those mentioned in Scripture. This means that there are limitations to the kind of pastoral response that is allowable within Roman Catholic doctrine.

Some contemporary online resources designed to help divorced Christians in this denomination, and those who counsel them, recommend an approach based on prayer and reflection first. This helps the individual to re-frame the divorce as a spiritual rather than emotional or practical challenge.

One example called *divorcedcatholic.com* advises a recovery program using a process akin to grief counselling and recommends readings that relate to the purpose of suffering in the world, as a path to finding peace with God. (See: **divorcedcatholic.com**, website run by Vince Frese, which recommends Peter Kreeft, *Making Sense out of Suffering.*)

This underlines the finality of marriage breakdown in Roman Catholic theology. In a related book, the owner of this website also recommends the use of Niehbuhr's famous "Serenity Prayer" which implies that true happiness is not attainable, but urges the believer to live "*Accepting hardships as the pathway to peace; … Trusting that He will make things right if I surrender to His Will; That I may be reasonably happy in this life and supremely happy with him for ever in the next*". (Cited in Duffy and Frese, *Divorced. Catholic. Now What?* p. 46.)

In summary, the Roman Catholic Church does not allow divorce on any grounds, and the only possible avenue of annulment brings its own problems by de-legitimising a first marriage and any children from that marriage.

Moreover, Roman Catholic Christians are condemned to spiritual isolation and long-term suffering with no hope of any release until death, unless of course, they reject the Church's teaching and live a double life, or alternatively choose to leave the Church altogether.

There are signs that this hard-line position may be slowly changing. In the meantime, the impact of divorce on Roman Catholic families is profoundly negative, with serious spiritual implications due to the connotations of failure and sinfulness which follow marriage break-up within this denominational context.

Chapter SIX: Liberal Perspectives

Scriptural Basis

Liberal approaches to the Gospel sources that deal with the issue of divorce often emphasise the historical context in which statements are made. Adrian Thatcher, who has written extensively on Christian marriage, divorce and related issues, argues that there are many Old Testament models of marriage based on the Jewish notion of the covenant. (Source: Thatcher, *Marriage after Modernity: Christian Marriage in Postmodern Times*, p. 68.)

The marriage covenant is modelled in God's covenant with Israel because the Hebrew word *davaq,* although translated as "united to" means "covenanted to." In Genesis 2:24 *"That is why a man leaves his father and mother and is* **covenanted to** *his wife, and they become one flesh"* (emphasis mine). However, Thatcher also points out a problem with the Old Testament teachings, in so far as *"women are stereotyped as inferior and unfaithful partners, a caricature upheld and reaffirmed many times over in Christianity"*. (Ibid., p. 69.)

This asymmetrical nature of the covenant concept raises questions about how applicable Old Testament models of marriage can be in modern times.

Gundry, *Heirs Together* and Howell, *Equality and Submissio* *in Marriage*, both argue for equal partnership in marriage. Eve modern evangelical authors accept that a partnership model fc marriage is more appropriate than a strictly patriarchal mode (For further reading, refer to Jong and Wilson, *Husband an Wife: The Sexes in Scripture and Society.*)

In the Gospels, it is evident that the Pharisees started discussion on divorce to test Jesus, thereby forcing Him t position Himself against contemporary political and religiou authority.

It has been noted, for example, that *"the question of the legali of divorce and remarriage had become politically hot since Joh the Baptist had publicly rebuked Herod Antipas for divorcing h wife to marry Herodias, the wife of this brother whom she ha divorced"*. (Source: Richmond, Garland and Garland, *Beyon Companionship: Christians in Marriage* p. 158.)

In other words, this context shows that Jesus is not choosing start a debate about divorce and its implications, but merel responding to the questions being put to Him. As Gardner an Gardner explain: *"Jesus was less concerned with marriage an kinship ties than with membership in the family of God."* (Ibid p. 172.)

It has been suggested that the teaching approach taken by Jesus in the Gospels is based on the Wisdom tradition of Jewish scholarship, which means that many deep truths are presented *in the form of proverbs, riddles, parables, allegories and the like ... there is a point to be understood from the teachings, but the point is a principle or a guideline not an absolute law to be followed exactly for all times and all places.* (See James M. Efird, *Marriage and Divorce: What the Bible Says,* pp. 38-39.)

Such an approach allows for interpretations that make allowances for human frailty in marital relationships, while still maintaining the goal of pure and lifelong marriage. The story of Jesus meeting the Samaritan woman at the well in John 4:1-30 and the woman caught in the act of adultery in John 8:1-11 are also evidence that Jesus did not reject those who had sinned but asked instead that those who accuse others should look to their own sinfulness.

Liberal interpretations of the instruction "*Go now and leave your life of sin*" in John 8:11 see this as an invitation to start afresh, without any clear directive on exactly how this can be achieved. Forster notes that *Jesus' approach was pastoral rather than legalistic when he was dealing with the needs of an individual whom he met. This approach looked forward rather than back.* (Source: Forster, *Healing Love's Wounds: A Pastoral Approach to Divorce and Remarriage* p. 59.)

If divorce is allowed, as it surely was in Jewish culture, then an adulterous situation can be remedied either by a return to the rightful marriage relationship, or by formal divorce proceedings and a fresh start for all concerned. Either way affected parties need to recognize the wrongs that have been done in the past and embrace a spirit of repentance.

Historical Tradition

An interesting debate on the interpretation of several Old Testament texts about marriage and divorce was instigated on Henry VIII's frustration with the Catholic Church's refusal to grant him a divorce from his first wife, Catherine.

Dr John Stokesly, Bishop of London from 1530 to 1539, helped to prepare a theological argument supporting the annulment of that marriage despite the Latin Vulgate version of Leviticus 18:16 which contains the clear statement "*Nobody may marry his brother's wife*". (Source: Chibi, '*Turpidudinem uxoris fratris tui non revelavit*': John Stokesly and the Divorce Question, p. 390.)

Henry VIII had obtained a dispensation from Pope Julius II to overcome this impediment, but Stokesly argued that dispensations could not overrule Divine law. This rendered the Pope's permission to marry invalid, and the marriage was therefore also null and void.

Furthermore, there are contradictory passages in the Old Testament, some commanding a man to marry his brother's wife on the death of the brother, and others forbidding it, and Stokesly explained this in terms of a distinction between Divine laws, which were absolute, and judicial rules which applied to the context of the Jewish people in their context but did not have any real moral authority beyond that time and place. (Chibi, p. 395.)

This nuanced approach to the theology behind marriage and divorce marks a departure from the Roman Catholic position and raises serious doubts about the authority of the Pope.

As the example of Henry VIII's disputes with the Roman Catholic Church has shown, the historical tradition of Christianity has often relied upon a thoughtful consideration of the context in which various doctrines emerged. For example, the liberal approach to divorce taken by the early Church is explained in terms of the concept of divorce as practised by citizens of the Roman Empire, which was seen as a private matter governed by the laws of contract. (See Snuth, *Divorce and Remarriage from the Early Church to John Wesley*, p. 131.)

Later, the strict rules of the reformed churches led to a separation of the process of divorce from the church in many countries, and the creation of secular divorce proceedings either through the courts, or through royal decree, as in the cases of Sweden and Switzerland.

(Source: Wiesner-Hanks, *Christianity and Sexuality in the Early Modern World: Regulating Desire, Reforming Practice*. p. 99.)

More recently liberal Christian churches have developed their understanding of the need to support divorcing and divorced couples and their families.

The work of liberal theologian Adrian Thatcher has done much to explore the implications of a society, including Christians, in which many people are in a "liminal state" in so far as they live at the edges of the accepted norm of lifelong marriage (See Thatcher, *Living Together and Christian*, p. 256.)

This group, which is very large in many modern societies includes people who are cohabiting before marriage, and those who are divorced.

Thatcher argues that a judgmental response to divorce in many churches has immediately negative consequences since *"divorced people may feel that in the eyes of the churches, their lives have already shown signs of irregularity and failure, so religious affiliation weakens or vanishes"*. (Ibid., p. 17.)

There is tremendous pressure on Christians from a surrounding society that operates according to a "post-Christian sexual ethic" which marginalizes marriage and replaces the idea of lifelong union with a more individualistic search for romantic love and evolving personal identity over the course of a whole lifetime. (Thatcher, *Marriage after* Modernity, pp. 60-61.)

Current Doctrine

The Anglican position on divorce has undergone many changes at both national and international levels, with some decisions on the grounds for divorce, and in some cases remarriage after divorce, being revised back and forth from the more conservative end of the spectrum to the more liberal end as different factions within the broad Anglican community gain and lose influence at the Synod level.

The current position is summed up on the Church of England website with a statement affirming the life-long intention of marriage along with a concession on the reality of marriage breakdown: *"The Church of England wishes all who marry a lifetime of love that grows within God's protection. But we recognise that some marriages do fail for all sorts of sad and painful reasons."* (The Church of England Divorce, p. 1.)

It is notable that this statement does not expressly limit the permissible grounds for divorce but makes a deliberately wide definition that could include issues beyond adultery and desertion mentioned in the Scriptures.

The Church of England's General Synod of July 2002 advised that "some marriages regrettably do fail and that the Church's care for couples in that situation should be of paramount importance." (Ibid., following the link *House of Bishops' Advice to the Clergy*, p. 1.)

This places responsibility for support squarely on the Church and implies that a focus on compassion rather than on the aspect of failure is uppermost in the minds of the ruling body of the Anglican Church in England.

Interestingly, the same Synod makes it clear that the decision whether to allow remarriage after divorce, even when the divorced partner is still living, is left to the individual priest who is asked to officiate at the second marriage. This decision rescinds earlier Canterbury and York convocations *which had exhorted clergy not to use the marriage service in the case of anyone who had a former partner still living.* (Ibid., p. 1.)

The implication of this ruling is that the Church has moved it position towards a more liberal acceptance of divorce as an unfortunate reality, while at the same time preserving conscience clause to allow clergy who do not agree with this move to retain their stricter interpretation of Scripture.

In practice, then, the Anglican Church offers a spectrum of positions, depending on the views of the local priest. Additionally, parishioners always have the option of consulting a different local leader if they feel that their pastor is not accepting of their position.

Impact on Families

Episcopalian author J. E. Adams argues that since divorce is not the unpardonable sin, it can be forgiven, but that this *does not heal all the heartbreaks of children and in-laws, not to speak of the parties involved in the divorce.* (Adams, *Marriage, Divorce and Remarriage in the Bible*: A Fresh Look at What Scripture Teaches. p. 25.)

One interesting empirical study explored the impact of divorce from Christians within a wide range of protestant denominations and found that despite the painful aspects of this experience, many people found it to be an opportunity for spiritual growth, resulting in greater appreciation of the love of God and of self and others in the Church. (See Blomquist, *The effect of the divorce experience on spiritual growth,* pp. 82-91.)

With appropriate pastoral support, many individuals who took part in this case study research were able to find their way to acceptance and forgiveness.

This included the ability to overcome the sense of failure they felt because their divorce was seen as falling short of the promises they had made to their partners and to God.

This is not to deny the seriousness of a failed marriage or its status as an undesirable turn of events, as compared with the norm set down by God in Scripture.

It is, however, a major concession to human frailty, and an invitation to let families work through the negative experience of divorce, starting from a position of forgiveness. They can then move forward with approval to begin rebuilding family life in new constellations which are somewhat different from the ideal, but nevertheless still accepted within the church community. Avenues of support are offered without judgement, and this forms the basis for healing for those who experience divorce in their families.

The Church of England website has created a notable policy and provided links to help Christians to access support from ecumenical groups, charities, and secular organizations, many of which have Christians in leadership positions. For further support you can visit the church website links to this charity for example: *Oneplusone: Strengthening relationships* (London: 2016) available at: http://www.oneplusone.org.uk/ .

This in turn has affiliations with The Tavistock Centre, the Terence Higgins Trust, and many other organizations.

This reflects a strong commitment to social action and a desire to collaborate with a wide range of other agencies who focus on the practical implications of divorce, rather than a narrow focus on theological interpretations.

There are also links to guide Christians on issues such as reducing the impact of divorce on children.

These guides are presented from the secular psychology viewpoint as opposed to focusing on a purely Christian perspective. One example is an article by Joanna Coker titled, *"How to reduce impact of divorce on children"* available at http://www.oneplusone.org.uk/blog/joanna-coker-how-to-reduce-impact-of-divorce-on-children/.

Chapter SEVEN: Evangelical Perspectives

Scriptural Basis

One very useful examination of the various mentions of divorce in the New Testament from an evangelical perspective compares two statements Jesus made. The first is recorded in Mark 10:11, "*Anyone who divorces his wife and marries another woman commits adultery against her.*" The longer version i from Matthew 19:9, "*I tell you that anyone who divorces his wife except for sexual immorality, and marries another woman commits adultery.*"

The evangelical perspective argues that the former version represents the actual words of Jesus, while the latter is a later addition by the author of the Gospel of Matthew who in fact used the Gospel of Mark as a source. (For further reading see Stein *Is it lawful for a man to divorce his wife?* p. 117.)

From this argument, the author concludes that there was no exception clause in the original words of Jesus, and the reason for this is that "*Jesus sought primarily to establish certain principles that would reveal the will of God to his listeners*" (Ibid., p. 119.)

In other words, this is a teaching about God's nature and the Divine will, rather than a lesson on the fine points of interpretation relating to Jewish law.

Another conservative evangelical commentary maintains that Jesus's teaching on marriage in Matthew 19:3-19 amounts to *"a radical refusal to recognize the validity of divorce."* (See France, *The Gospel According to Matthew: An Introduction and Commentary*, p. 123.)

Further evidence to support this conservative line of interpretation is found in apostle Paul's distinction between the general principle *"To the married I give this command (not I, but the Lord): a wife must not separate from her husband..."* (I Corinthians 7:10). This command comes with a concession to show that he accepts that some couples will not live up to this ideal *"but if she does, she must remain unmarried or else be reconciled to her husband."* (I Corinthians 7:11).

There is another concession mentioned in the case of an unbelieving husband or wife who leaves his or her partner, since Paul writes that *"the brother or sister is not bound in such circumstances; God has called us to live in peace."* (I Corinthians 7: 15). The full argument is given in Stein, pp. 117-120.

The evangelical perspective thus holds to a strict prohibition of divorce with only two exceptions namely adultery and the desertion of a non-Christian partner which leaves the innocer party free to divorce and then establish a Christian marriag with another person.

Historical Tradition

The Reformation has been an important force in shaping th Evangelical tradition regarding divorce. A key element of tha was the deliberate distancing of reformed churches from th practices of Roman Catholicism in social relations. The celibac rule was abolished, and in Calvin's Geneva, new rules wer established to regulate cases of infidelity or desertion of on party in a marriage, allowing for divorces in these restricte circumstances. (See Witte Jr. and Kingdon, *Sex, Marriage ar Family in John Calvin's Geneva*.)

Humanists including Erasmus and Thomas More, a Catholic also called for a review of the rules on divorce and started long debate in reformed churches that continues to this da (Source: Phillips, *Untying the Knot: A Short History of Divorce* pp. 11-12.)

In 1647 the Westminster Confession of Faith, which underpins the theology of the Presbyterian and some other reformed churches, stipulates the two scriptural concessions regarding desertion and adultery. It further emphasizes the duty of the Church to regulate the process of divorce, and the importance of dove-tailing church responses with the civil process:

> *Although the corruption of man be such as is apt to study arguments, unduly to put asunder those whom God hath joined together in marriage; yet nothing but adultery, or such wilful desertion as can no way be remedied by the church or civil magistrate, is cause sufficient of dissolving the bond of marriage: wherein a publick and orderly course of proceeding is to be observed, and the persons concerned in it not left to their own wills and discretion in their own case. (Source: The Westminster Confession of Faith (1647) Section 24.)*

One of the issues that has been highly discussed in the centuries since then is the meaning of Old Testament terms such as "covenant" which is a mainly moral/spiritual term and "contract" which is a more legal term.

They also seek ways in which they can both be used to define what divorce really means at any point in history. (See Instone-Brewer, *Divorce and Remarriage in the Bible.* pp. 18-19.)

An influential view from conservative evangelical theologian John Stott defines marriage as "*a sacred bond between a man and a woman instituted by and publicly entered into before God (whether or not this is acknowledged by the married couple), normally consummated by sexual intercourse.*" (Source: Stott, *Our Social and Sexual Revolution: Major Issues for a New Century*, p. 137.)

This is endorsed by some evangelical organizations and extends to a view that applies to everyone, not just committed Christians, holding that "*The Bible is clear that marriage is intended to be lifelong. This is for everyone's good irrespective of whether the married couple are Christians.*" (Source: The Christian Institute, "Marriage and the Family" p. 1.)

It suggests that even the concessions of divorce as a legitimate response in cases of adultery and desertion that are expressly permitted in Scripture do not apply to Catholic and Evangelical Christians.

Current Doctrine

Within Evangelical church communities there was until recently much less evidence that positions had softened at official levels than in the other two branches explored above.

One author claims that "*fundamentalist Protestant groups have been particularly concerned about the future of families, and some have taken strong traditional positions on role relations between men and women, abortion, and family stability*", including of course a negative position towards separation and divorce (Thornton, p. 858.)

An example of this hard-line approach to divorce can be found in American evangelical author Curtis Thomas's statement that "*In the case of either persistent porneia or desertion, the innocent party not only has the right to dissolve the marriage but is also free to remarry.*" (Thomas, *Practical Wisdom for Pastors: Words of Encouragement and Counsel for a Lifetime of Ministry*, p. 163.)

The quotation of the Greek word *porneia,* meaning sexual immorality alludes to the concession cited by Jesus in Matthew 19:9, and mentioned in Hebrews 14:4. (See Laney, "No Divorce and No Remarriage" in H. Wayne House (Ed.), *Divorce and Remarriage: Four Christian Views*, p. 34.)

However, there is no explanation of how a pastor can or should be able to determine which party is innocent and which is guilty. This appears to contradict the line that Jesus takes in prohibiting the practice of Christians judging other Christians.

In his commentary on Matthew's Gospel, Evans points out that when Jesus makes an appeal to the creation of man as male and female, referring to the Book of Genesis, he implies that "divorce is tantamount to an undoing of the created order." (Source: Craig A. Evans, *The Bible Knowledge Background Commentary: Matthew-Luke,* p. 347).

This, too, suggests that marriage is permanent, and that divorce is contrary to God's will. A similar position is taken in a book length study by Wenham and Heth, where divorce is seen as an absolute last resort, with no permission to remarry afterwards. (See Wenham and Heth, *Jesus and Divorce Towards an Evangelical Understanding of New Testament Teaching.*)

However, it is interesting that in an article written in 2002 Baptist author Heth explains how after much reflection and reading other evangelical theologians' views, he has changed his mind on this point, and joined with an emerging consensus that accepts divorce in an Evangelical Christian context, on the grounds that Biblical covenants can be broken.

This is in the light of exegesis of Paul's teachings that consider the context of the early Church. (Refer to Heth, "Jesus on Divorce: How My Mind Has Changed" *The Southern Baptist Journal of Theology* Vol, 6, pp. 4-29.)

Heth concedes that some points regarding the pastoral practicalities of divorce are difficult to determine from the sparse records of Scripture and acknowledges that a minority of evangelical Christians will insist on a hard-line interpretation of Paul's teachings but advises readers to rely upon *"one's theologically informed conscience"* when considering issues of debate such as remarriage after divorce. Ibid., p. 21.)

It appears, then, that there is quite a spectrum of perspectives within evangelical Christian churches ranging from absolute prohibition to tolerance for divorce in some circumstances.

One commentator notes that in the 1970s, when thanks to feminism and reforms in education, more women were taking up educational opportunities and participating in the labour market, contact with new ideas brought conflict with the more traditional values of some evangelical groups. (Source: Macrae, Jr., "The Secularization of Divorce.")

Yet another commentator notes: *Although evangelical an fundamentalist leaders are not inclined to look at divorce a morally neutral, as do some clergy and theologians, they a express a surprising range of opinions on the subject.* (Se Wilcox, Soft Patriarchs, New Men: How Christianity Shape Fathers and Husbands. p. 48.)

In Pentecostal Christianity there have been shifts towards more liberal attitude to divorce, to the extent that celebrit preachers such as Juanita Bynum and Paula White publicl announced their intention to divorce. (Van Biema, "A Evangelical Rethink on Divorce?" *TIME* p. 1.)

This debate has rumbled on through the end of the twentiet and start of the twenty-first century resulting in a gradual shift i evangelical circles which increasingly overlaps with the liber; perspective. (See Goddard, "Theology and Practices in th Evangelical Churches.")

Impact of Divorce on Families

It is difficult to draw any definite conclusions about the impac of evangelical perspectives on families experiencing divorce The impact of divorce on families among Evangelic; communities mostly depends upon where each community lie within the spectrum of tolerance for divorce.

Some families experience isolation and exclusion like that found in the Roman Catholic Church. In other scenarios, the compassion and forgiveness that is present in more tolerant evangelical communities will be available to them.

In *Evangelical Presbyterian Churches, "Divorce and Remarriage"*, the Presbyterian denomination expressly states:

> *We believe that congregations within the Evangelical Presbyterian Church can take many helpful steps to minister the redemptive love of Christ to their members who go through the tragedy of divorce, and to reach out to those outside the Church who are suffering the aftermath of divorce.* (Source: *http://www.epc.org/positionpapers*)

This positioning of divorce as an opportunity for compassion and evangelism shows that a strong focus on the covenant of marriage is not incompatible with a genuine commitment to welcome those whose marriage has failed for whatever reason.

The same document also recommends a divorce recovery program organized by the church to set out a pathway so that *such realities as guilt, resentment, frustration, fear and anger resulting from the first marriage are not carried over as a time bomb to destroy the second marriage.* (p. 10.)

This practical suggestion offers a way to deal with the impact of divorce that does not let such families be classed as "*second class Christians.*" In his book, *Second Class Christians? A New Approach to the Dilemma of Divorced Persons in the Church*, A. Michael emphasizes the Church's work in healing fractured lives.

The same theology of faith-based redemption and forgiveness which does not focus on past actions, can offer a way to lessen the negative impact of divorce for families and structure a way back to healthy and loving relationships within the fellowship of other Christians. A similar view is also suggested by Bruce Parmenter in *Christians Caught in the Divorce Trap: Helping Families Recover from Divorce*.

Chapter EIGHT: Theological and Pastoral Reflection

Theological Reflection

It is clear from the varied positions outlined above that many issues relating to divorce and its impact on Christian families remain contentious. One outcome from this study's research has been the realisation that the Christian authors from the three main branches of Christianity cited above each produce some widely differing conclusions despite all drawing on the same passages of Scripture such as Matthew 19:3-12, Mark 10:2-12 and I Corinthians 7:12-16.

However, in starting to reflect theologically about this puzzling tension it was important for me to recognise that many of the most contentious points arise out of the different contexts surrounding the various interpretations made from these same scriptural texts. Terms like "*become one flesh*" or "*fornication*" and "*adultery*" can be defined in different ways, and in my view, the reason for that lies in the norms that are set down by each social group in different places and at different points in history.

All the theologians discussed above affirm the normative nature of lifelong marriage as a structure for living which reflects God's creation of the world and His covenant with His people.

There is also a universal recognition that many people do not live up to this norm or ideal, and that divorce as a secular legally binding process, is a reality that is becoming more common within modern society.

In reflecting on these issues, I noticed that some differences have crept into Christian theology through the way in which these texts become formalised into institutional policies. In most cases there has been a focus on defining the nature of the failure and meting out consequences on those who find themselves affected by divorce, sometimes even with an implication that one party is guilty and the other innocent. While there is always a high level of guilt and suffering for all concerned, this affects people most severely in the more conservative churches.

Historical events, usually involving kings and rulers, have pushed theologians to make arguments that support, or resist particular positions on the pro- or anti-divorce camps. Gender politics has certainly influenced some denominational positions also, and some of the movement towards more equality within marriage is evidence of the influence of feminism.

However, politics is all about the power that human beings wield over one another. In the vast literature on divorce within Christianity, the focus is mostly on the position of bishops and clergy, advising them on how to deal administratively with the impact of divorce on adults, notably those who wish to remarry after divorce.

What is much less evident in the many books and articles that I have read on this topic, is a focus on the weak and the poor: including children whose lives are affected by divorce, and grandparents, aunts and uncles who may lose touch with the children in their families through divorce. Spiritual effects such as isolation from God and from the supportive environment of a local church community are also very serious leading to a loss of faith for many individuals, and a backlog of hurt and despair that affects them for the rest of their lives.

It is as if the Church through the ages has tried to contain the problem of divorce by reinforcing one single ideal of lifelong marriage and excluding those who cannot live up to this ideal.

This results in many contradictory situations where theologians are forced either to get round the Gospel prohibition on divorce through concepts such as annulment, or to devise carefully defined concessions through creative interpretation of contentious biblical words.

Key Insights

In Divorce and Remarriage: Four Christian Views, Hous suggests a new way of looking at these issues and asks, "*Ho does God's Word affect this issue? Where and how does God forgiveness come into play?*

Several key insights have arisen from studying the issue c divorce and its impact on Christian families. The first of thes has been the existing gaps and overlaps between th approaches offered by scientific writings in the fields c sociology and psychology on the one hand, and the approache offered within the three main Christian branches examine above.

This disparity prompted me to reflect further on the commo goals of human and Divine endeavour to bring wholeness t individual lives and the wider society. Reading more about th origins of modern sociology in Christian thinking, I discovere that at the very start of sociological theory in the 1890s i Chicago, two of the key thinkers in these fields, including Albic W. Small and Graham Taylor were Christians who saw n conflict between their theories and their Protestant Christia faith (see Henking, "Sociological Christianity and Christia Sociology: The Paradox of Early American Sociology" *Religic and American Culture: A Journal of Interpretation*, pp. 49-67.)

Christianity was seen as the solution to the many ills of modern urban society such as poverty, intemperance, immigration, industrial exploitation and labour difficulties (Ibid., p. 55).

However, there is little mention of divorce in their work, and with the passage of time the focus of sociology has diverged somewhat from the core tenets of Christian belief.

More recent scientific work focusing on the impact of divorce on people with different ethnic and religious views has shown that the negative effect of divorce on families *"is stronger in countries that have stronger norms against divorce, but this was only found for religious persons."* (Source: Kalmijn, "Country Differences in the Effects of Divorce on Well-Being: The Role of Norms, Support, and Selectivity" p. 475.)

This is a sobering finding which suggests that Christians are suffering more than non-Christians when they experience divorce. It suggests also that there is more that Christian communities should be doing to help those in their midst who are experiencing divorce.

Pastoral Reflection

It was important to explore the theology behind different teachings on divorce and the history of different church positions because this has helped to clarify when and why different denominations have adopted their individual perspectives.

A good summary is presented in *Religious Tolerance, "The range of religious views on divorce and remarriage"*. (Source: http://www.religioustolerance.org/chr_divo.htm)

However, it is even more important to understand the impact of these positions on Christian families, and to put together theory and practice in a way that is both scriptural and positively helpful in the modern world. Within the Roman Catholic and strictly Evangelical branches of the Church there is a sense of hopelessness, both in the families where divorce has occurred, and in the pastors charged with ministering to those affected.

The consequences of divorce are invariably negative, involving feelings of failure and rejection, and a social stigma that blights children and grandparents as well as divorcing couples themselves.

There is a sense among the more conservative perspectives that the wrongs of the past cannot be put right.

Furthermore, those who suffer divorce can never regain peace with themselves, their former partners, and their church community because they are forever labelled as failures. Legalistic pastoral responses add more pain and suffering in a situation that is already extremely difficult for most people.

The Internet provides many testimonials from people who have been traumatised by rejection in childhood because of their parents' divorce, as Kathy notes in "The Worst Rejection." Further evidence is shared by those who divorce and find themselves isolated and without support because of negative and judgmental pastoral responses.

At this point I ask myself whether it is more important to preserve the purity of a single interpretation of Scripture among many, or to meet the needs of people who are in great distress, crying out for the Church's support and God's saving grace.

I look to Paul's example, who was often found in the position of having to make rulings on contentious issues that arose in the early church settlements that were grappling with these issues without the benefit of centuries of prior thinking to help them resolve immediate dilemmas.

It is noticeable that Paul follows the example of Jesus and the Gospel writers. He often cites a general principle which is clearly the ideal God sets for people to adhere to.

This is followed by some concession or other that deals with the individual local situation that has arisen to cause consternation within a particular community. In 1 Corinthians 7 for example, it is noticeable that "*on virtually every subtopic of his discussion Paul offers an exception or qualification of his command or opinion.*" as Horsley notes in *Abingdon New Testament Commentaries: I Corinthians* (p. 96).

This shows that pastoral workers must consider the reality of human sin and the needs of each community as presented in its own unique situation. While the eternal truths and ideals do not change, Christians are subject to ever-changing problems and challenges, and look to their Christian leaders for guidance on how to deal with these harsh realities.

The words of liberal theologian Greg Forster have helped me to formulate my own position on these difficult issues. I found it helpful to read this considered conclusion on the exegetical difficulties of the Gospel accounts:

"I believe that Jesus was teaching his followers not just what to think, but how to think ethically, so that they could then come to their own conscientious decisions. Whereas the Jewish lawyers were arguing over the niceties of procedure, and the precise meaning of words in Deuteronomy 24, he pushed them back to why God instituted marriage." (Forster, *"The Changing Face of Marriage and Divorce"*, p. 176).

By trying to work out what Scripture commands, what is allowed as a concession, and where exactly the boundary between the two might lie, we might be falling into the same trap as the Pharisees who insisted on defining the letter of the law, rather than meeting the needs of people who fail. They are still seeking to follow God and also relieve their own suffering and that of their families.

Mercy, forgiveness, and compassion for sinners need not be seen as ways of condoning sin, but rather as ways of recognising where things have gone wrong, learning from these mistakes, and helping people to set up a new direction in their lives that lead to a more stable and positive place. As Geisler writes *"Jesus condemned those who exalted laws at the expense of lives."* (See Norman, *Christian Ethics: Contemporary Issues and Options*, p. 309.)

Given the seriously negative spiritual, emotional, social an often financial consequences that divorced couples and the families experience, it is surely our pastoral duty to help peopl look to the future rather than focus on the painful past. Som helpful literature is available on the experience that committe Christians have had both during and after divorce, including th difficult issue of how to deal with ex-partners during a secon marriage. (See Houck and Houck, *The Ex Factor: Dealing wi Your Former Spouse*).

In pastoral work, there is an urgent need to offer support an encouragement to all Christians, and especially those who ar experiencing any kind of life crisis, which of course includes th experience of divorce. Legalistic views drive people away fror God, while a more holistic view in terms of God's will for th Church and His love for those who just cannot live up to H standards consistently will draw people to God.

There are many concessions in the various biblical texts. Thos who interpret Scripture literally must concede that thes concessions relate to the specific social and political contex1 in which the Jewish and Christian believers lived. Our moder world has its own pressures, and we desperately nee theologians and pastors who can teach the ideals, while havin compassion for those who have failed and want to start afres with forgiveness and peace in their hearts.

While studying this topic it has become clear to me that the problem of divorce is part of a much bigger field which I would more generally define as relationships. Marriage and divorce take place within a network of other relationships, including a relationship with God, with members of the nuclear and extended family, and with the Church. I see the requirement for pastoral work as a duty that covers all these dimensions at the same time.

The impact of divorce can be very severe for many families, and if a Christian community is open and welcoming to people experiencing marital difficulties, then it has a greater chance of preventing divorce through early interventions such as counselling. It can offer concrete support during crisis, using referrals to secular and charity agencies as well as in-house church members of staff. The Christian community can further offer compassion and hope to those who have gone through the emotionally and spiritually draining experience of divorce.

It is abundantly clear to me that the support of children is very difficult if one or both parents are ostracised by the Church community. The danger of whole families losing faith completely and removing themselves from the beneficial influence of the pastor and the church is high if there is no hope of full participation in the spiritual life of the Church after divorce.

In my view, we have a duty to situate divorce within the wider framework of a loving and forgiving God, and a supportive Christian fellowship which assists those who have sinned, and those who suffer without judging them. We have all sinned and we have all failed. This is no reason to exclude divorced people from the grace of God and the gift of fellowship with Him and His people.

Chapter NINE: Conclusion and Recommendations

Conclusion

This research has reviewed past and present theology on the issue of divorce and provided some understanding of the background that underpins the differing responses Christian churches have developed over the centuries. This knowledge has also formed the basis of theological reflection on past and current doctrine and the impacts that different policies are currently having on Christian families, including divorcing couples, their children, and other members of their extended family.

From the above discussion, no great difference exists in the starting point for their thinking. However, different branches of the Church differ in their conclusions either because they interpret the scriptural extracts differently or because they give different weightings to the various passages that they use.

There is universal support for the lifelong nature of marriage as God intended it.

Additionally, in recent years there has been a gradual realization that divorce is a reality in a fallen world, and a growing acceptance that Christians have a duty to help people recover from it rather than compound their suffering in an already traumatic situation.

Recommendations

It is acknowledged that given the diversity of approaches that have existed through the ages, and to some extent still prevail across the world, it is unlikely that a single, coherent position on how best to counsel and support Christian families will emerge

In the end the pastoral dilemmas caused by divorce come down to an inherent tension between revealed theology from biblical times, man-made, historical practices through the ages, and the contemporary need to show compassion to those who fail and help them find their way to recovery from the negative impacts of such a serious breakdown in relationships.

This means that for Church workers in every denomination there is never going to be one simple and universally agreed pastoral response to divorce. Individual cases differ, church rules evolve, and each local Christian community has its own set of variables depending on historical viewpoints and the personalities who have authority and power within the community.

Despite this complexity, it is possible to highlight some key principles or objectives that can guide pastoral workers in how to deal with the impact of divorce.

Principle One: Prevention

Principle Two: Support in a crisis

Principle Three: Coming to terms with the reality of divorce

Principle Four: Restoring spiritual connection with God

Principle Five: Overcoming guilt

Principle Six: Healing of family relationships

Principle Seven: Rebuilding full fellowship with the Church

Jesus advised that "*My yoke is easy and My burden is light*" (Mt. 11:28-29) and expressly recommended that people come to Him when they are weary and burdened.

There is no tolerance of willful disobedience found in the Gospels, but there is always a way of forgiveness and healing for those who have failed, who acknowledge that failure, and who come to Jesus in a spirit of humility and repentance. The path of recovery from divorce must necessarily be quite long and will often be very hard.

If pastors follow these principles faithfully, and as far as they can within the limits of their denominational rules, then they will have the best basis for a compassionate and healing response to the modern problem of divorce in Christian families.

This could further provide the basis for building greate
ecumenical unity, where necessary identifying some areas c
focus for future prayer and reflection, so that Christians livin
and working in different denominations can better serve the
communities.

About the Author

Reverend Walter Orinda holds a master's degree in theology from the University of Roehampton UK (2016). He is a compassionate researcher and mentor with a commitment to nurture unity and growth in family and ministry.

The author is the senior Pastor at New Life Destiny Baptist Church in West Drayton, Harmondsworth serving with his loving wife Pastor Lillian Orinda.

They are blessed with wonderful children.

Connect at:

YouTube: @newlifedestinybaptistchurch1

Bibliography

The following bibliography includes References by Chapter, Primary Sources, and Secondary Literature.

Reference by Chapter:

Chapter One: God's Purpose for Marriage

Holy Bible, New King James Version, (Genesis 2:18-24)

Ibid, Ephesians 5:25-33.

Chapter Two: Marriage Structures

Balswick, Jack O. and Balswick, Judith K., *The Family: A Christian Perspective on the Contemporary Home.* Third edition. (Grand Rapids, MI: Baker Academic, 2007), p. 15.

Moxnes, Halvor., "What is family? Problems in constructing early Christian families. In Halvor Moxnes, (Ed.), *Constructing Early Christian Families: Family as Social Reality and Metaphor* (London: Psychology Press, 1997), pp. 13-15.)

Weitzman, Lenore, *The Divorce Revolution.* (New York: Free Press, 1985).

Demo, David H .and Acock, Alan C., "The Impact of Divorce upon Children," *Journal of Marriage and Family* Vol. 50, No. 3, pp. 619-648.

Amato, Paul R., "Research on Divorce: Continuing Trends and New Developments," *Journal of Marriage and Family* Vol. 72, No. 3, (2010) pp. 650-666.

Chapter Three: Scope of the Study

Grunlan, Stephen A., *Marriage and the Family: A Christian Perspective*. Revised edition. (Grand Rapids, MI: Zondervan, 1999), p. 223.

Amato, Paul R. and Keith, Bruce., "Parental Divorce and the Well-Being of Children: A Meta-Analysis," *Psychological Bulletin* Vol. 110, No. 1 (1991), pp. 26-46; Paul R. Amato, "The consequences of divorce for adults and children," *Journal of Marriage and Family* Vol. 62, No. 4 (2000), pp. 1269-1287; Andrew Root, *The Children of Divorce: The Loss of Family as the Loss of Being* (Grand Rapids, MI: Baker Academic, 2010).

Ibid., p. 26.

Teachman, Jay, D. and Paasch, Kathleen M. *The Future of Children* Vol. 4, No. 1 (1994), pp. 63-83.

Fagan, Patrick F. and Churchill, Aaron., *The Effects of Divorce on Children: Research Synthesis*. (Washington, DC: Marriage & Religion Research Institute, 1999).

Amato, Paul R.; Booth, Alan.; Johnson, David R. and Rogers, Stacy J. *Alone Together: How Marriage in America is Changing.* (Cambridge, MA: Harvard University Press, 2007), p. 181.

Segal, Robert A. "In Defense of the Comparative Method" *Numen* Vol. 48, No. 3, p. 339.

Chapter Five: Roman Catholic Perspective

Genesis 2:24.

Deuteronomy 24:1-4.

Jones, David Clyde., "A Note on the LXX of Malachi 2:16" *Journal of Biblical Literature* Vol. 109, No. 4, (1990), p. 683.

Ibid., pp. 683-684.

Matthew 19:9.

Fiorenza, Francis Schüssler., "Marriage". In Francis Schüssler Fiorenza (Ed.), *Systematic Theology: Roman Catholic Perspectives.* Second edition. Minneapolis, MN: Fortress Press, p. 616.

Ibid., pp. 617-618.

The Canons and Decrees of the Sacred and Oecumenical Council of Trent in J. Waterworth (Trans. and Ed), (London: Dolman, 1848) [originally in Latin in 1563). Available at: **http://history.hanover.edu/texts/trent.html** [Accessed 6 February 2016].

Catechism of the Catholic Church. Second edition. (Rome: Vatican, 2015), para 2384. Available at: **http://www.usccb.org/beliefs-and-teachings/what-we-believe/catechism/catechism-of-the-catholic-church/epub/index.cfm** [Accessed 6 February 2016].

Onedera, Jill D. "The Practice of Marriage and Family Counseling and Catholicism" in Jill Duba Onedera (Ed.), *The Role of Religion in Marriage and Family Counseling* (London and New York: Routledge, 2008), pp. 46-47.

Fiorenza, p. 616.

Lawlor, Michael., *Marriage and the Catholic Church*: Disputed Questions (Collegeville, MN: Liturgical Press, 2002).

Goodstein, Laurie and Povoledo, Elisabeta., "Amid Splits, Catholic Bishops Crack Open Door on Divorce" *New York Times* (24 October 2015), p. 1. Available at: **http://www.nytimes.com/2015/10/25/world/europe/synod-makes-overture-to-the-divorced-but-rejects-gay-marriage.html** [Accessed 6 February 2016].

Pope Francis, cited in Elizabeth Scalia, *Pope Francis's quiet campaign to rethink divorce in the Catholic Church,* The Guardian (5 February 2014), p. 1. Available at: **http://www.theguardian.com/commentisfree/2014/feb/05/pope-francis-catholic-church-divorce-change** [Accessed 6 February 2016].

Lisa, Duffy., "7 ways Parish Leaders Can Better Serve Divorced Catholics". (1 August 2015) Available at: **http://www.catholicmatch.com/institute/2015/08/5-ways-parish-leaders-can-better-serve-divorced-catholics/** [Accessed 6 February 2016].

Thornton, Arland. "Changing Attitudes toward Separation and Divorce: Causes and Consequences" *American Journal of Sociology* Vol. 90, No. 4, (1985), p. 858.

House, H. Wayne (Ed.), *Divorce and Remarriage: Four Christian Views* (Downers Grove, IL: InterVarsity Press, 1990

Message of the XI Ordinary General Assembly of the Synod c Bishops. (Rome: Vatican, 2005) Available at: **http://www.vatican.va/roman_curia/synod/documents/rc_ ynod_doc_20051022_message-synod_en.html** [Accessed February 2016], para. 15.

divorcedcatholic.com (website run by Vince Frese) [Accessed 6 February 2016]

Duffy, Lisa and Frese, Vince., *Divorced. Catholic. Now What?* Third edition. (Marietta, CA: Journey of Hope Productions, 2011), p. 46.

Chapter Six: Liberal Perspectives

Thatcher, Adrian., *Marriage after Modernity: Christian Marriage in Postmodern Times* (New York: New York University Press, 1999), p. 68.

Ibid., p. 69.

Gundry, Patricia., *Heirs Together* (Grand Rapids: Zondervan, 1980) and John C. Howell, *Equality and Submission in Marriage* (Nashville: Broadman, 1979).

De Jong, Peter and Wilson, Donald R. *Husband and Wife: The Sexes in Scripture and Society* (Grand Rapids, MI: Zondervan, 1979).

Garland, Diana S. Richmond, and Garland, David E. *Beyond Companionship: Christians in Marriage* (Eugene, OR: Wipf and Stock, 2003), p. 158.

Ibid., p. 172.

James M. Efird, *Marriage and Divorce: What the Bible Says* (Eugene, OR: Wipf and Stock, 2001), pp. 38-39.

Forster, Greg., *Healing Love's Wounds: A Pastoral Approach to Divorce and Remarriage* (Grand Rapids, MI: Zondervan, 1995), p. 59.

Chibi, Andrew A. '*Turpidudinem uxoris fratris tui non revelavit*': John Stokesly and the Divorce Question, *Sixteenth Century Journal* Vol. 25, No. 2 (1994), p. 390.

Ibid., p. 395.

Snuth, David L. "Divorce and Remarriage from the Early Church to John Wesley" *Trinity Journal* Vol. 11, No. 2 (1990), p. 131.

Wiesner-Hanks, Merry., *Christianity and Sexuality in the Early Modern World: Regulating Desire, Reforming Practice*. Second edition. (Abingdon: Routledge, 2010), p. 99.

Thatcher, Adrian, *Living Together and Christian Ethics* (Cambridge: Cambridge University Press, 2002), p. 256.

Ibid., p. 17.

Thatcher, Adrian., *Marriage after* Modernity, pp. 60-61.

The Church of England Divorce (2016) Available at: **https://www.churchofengland.org/our-views/marriage,-family-and-sexuality-issues/divorce.aspx** [Accessed 6 February 2016], p. 1.

Ibid., following the link *House of Bishops' Advice to the Clergy*, p. 1.

Ibid., p. 1.

Adams, Jay E. Marriage, Divorce and Remarriage in the Bible: A Fresh Look at What Scripture Teaches. (Grand Rapids, MI: Zondervan, 1980), p. 25.

Blomquist, Jean M. "The effect of the divorce experience on spiritual growth" Pastoral Psychology Vol. 34, No. 2, (1985), pp. 82-91.

Oneplusone: Strengthening relationships (London: 2016) Available at: **http://www.oneplusone.org.uk/** [Accessed 6 February 2016].

Coker, Joanna, "How to reduce impact of divorce on children". (London: oneplusone, 2014). Available at: **http://www.oneplusone.org.uk/blog/joanna-coker-how-to-reduce-impact-of-divorce-on-children/** [Accessed 6 February 2016].

Chapter Seven: Evangelical Perspectives

Stein, Robert H. "Is it lawful for a man to divorce his wife?" *Journal of the Evangelical Theological Society* Vol. 22, No. 2, p. 117.

Ibid., p. 119.

France, R. T. *The Gospel According to Matthew: An Introduction and Commentary* (Leicester: InterVarsity Press, 1985), p. 123.

I Corinthians 7:10.

I Corinthians 7:11.

I Corinthians 7: 15. The full argument is given in Stein, pp. 117-120.

Witte Jr, John and Kingdon, Robert M. *Sex, Marriage and Family in John Calvin's Geneva* (Grand Rapids, MI: Eerdmans, 2005).

Phillips, Roderick., *Untying the Knot: A Short History of Divorce* (Cambridge: Cambridge University Press, 1991), pp. 11-12.

The Westminster Confession of Faith (1647) Section 24. **http://www.reformed.org/documents/wcf_with_proofs/** [Accessed 6 February 2016].

Instone-Brewer, David., *Divorce and Remarriage in the Bible.* (Grand Rapids: Eerdmans, 2002)., pp. 18-19.

Stott, John., Our Social and Sexual Revolution: Major Issues for a New Century (Grand Rapids: Baker, 1999), p. 137.

The Christian Institute, "Marriage and the Family" (Newcastle Upon Tyne, 2016), p. 1. Available at: **http://www.christian.org.uk/resources/theology/apologetic s/marriage-and-family/divorce/** [Accessed 6 February 2016].

Thornton, p. 858.

Thomas, Curtis C. *Practical Wisdom for Pastors: Words of Encouragement and Counsel for a Lifetime of Ministry* (Wheaton, IL: Crossway, 2001), p. 163.

Laney, J. Carl, "No Divorce and No Remarriage" in H. Wayne House (Ed.), *Divorce and Remarriage: Four Christian Views* (Downers Grove, IL: InterVarsity Press, 1990), p. 34.

Evans, Craig A., *The Bible Knowledge Background Commentary: Matthew-Luke* (Eastbourne: Kingsway Communications, 2003), p. 347.

Wenham, Gordon J. and Heth, William E. *Jesus and Divorce: Towards an Evangelical Understanding of New Testament Teaching.* Second edition. (Carlisle: Paternoster, 1997).

Heth, William A. "Jesus on Divorce: How My Mind Has Changed" *The Southern Baptist Journal of Theology* Vol, 6 (2002), pp. 4-29.

Ibid., p. 21.

James A. Macrae, Jr., "The Secularization of Divorce", in Beverly Duncan and Otis Dudly Duncan (Eds.), *Sex Typing and Social Roles* (New York: Academic Press, 1978), pp. 227 – 242.

Wilcox, W. Bradford and Soft Patriarchs, New Men: How Christianity Shapes Fathers and Husbands (Chicago and London: University of Chicago Press, 2004), p. 48.

Van Biema, David., "An Evangelical Rethink on Divorce?" *TIME* (15 November, 2007), p. 1. Available at: **http://content.time.com/time/nation/article/0,8599,1680709, 00.html** [Accessed 6 February 2016].

Goddard, Andrew., "Theology and Practices in the Evangelical Churches" in Adrian Thatcher (Ed.), *The Oxford Handbook of Theology, Sexuality and Gender* (Oxford: Oxford University Press, 2014), p. 383.

Chapter Eight: Theological and Pastoral Reflection

Evangelical Presbyterian Churches, *"Divorce and Remarriage"* (Livonia, MI: Evangelical Presbyterian Churches: 1995), pp 9-10. Available at: **http://www.epc.org/positionpapers** [Accessed 6 February 2016].

Ibid, p. 10.

Michael, A., *Second Class Christians? A New Approach to the Dilemma of Divorced Persons in the Church (p1)*.

Parmenter, Bruce., *Christians Caught in the Divorce Trap: Helping Families Recover from Divorce* (Joplin, MO: College Press Publishing Company).

House, H. Wayne., Introduction. In H. Wayne House (Ed.), *Divorce and Remarriage: Four Christian Views* (Downers Grove, IL: InterVarsity Press, 1990), p. 11.

Henking. Susan E., "Sociological Christianity and Christian Sociology: The Paradox of Early American Sociology" *Religion and American Culture: A Journal of Interpretation* Vol. 3, No. 1 (1993), pp. 49-67.

Ibid., p. 55.

Kalmijn, Matthijs., "Country Differences in the Effects of Divorce on Well-Being: The Role of Norms, Support, and Selectivity" *European Sociological Review,* Vol. 26, no. 4 (2010), p. 475.

Religious Tolerance, *"The range of religious views on divorce and remarriage"*. Ontario: Religious Tolerance, 2015. Available: **http://www.religioustolerance.org/chr_divo.htm** [Accessed 6 Februrary 2016].

Kathy S., "The Worst Rejection" (2016). Available at: **http://whosoever.org/v5i2/quinn.html** [Accessed 6 February 2016]

Horsley, Richard A., *Abingdon New Testament Commentaries: I Corinthians* (Nashville, TX: Abingdon Press, 1998), p. 96.

Forster, Greg., "The Changing Face of Marriage and Divorce" Anvil Vol. 17, No. 3, (2000), p. 176.

Norman, L., *Christian Ethics: Contemporary Issues and Options*. Second edition. (Grand Rapids, MI: Baker Publishing Group, 2010), p. 309.

Houck, Don and Houck, LaDean., *The Ex Factor: Dealing with Your Former Spouse* (Grand Rapids, MI: Revell, 1997).

Matthew 11:28-29.

Note: Unless otherwise stated, references to the Bible are from the New International Version (NIV). Available at: **https://www.biblegateway.com/** [Accessed 6 February 2016].

Primary Sources (includes journalistic texts and websites)

Catechism of the Catholic Church. Second edition. (Rome: Vatican, 2015). Available at: **http://www.usccb.org/beliefs-and-teachings/what-we-believe/catechism/catechism-of-the-catholic-church/epub/index.cfm** [Accessed 6 February 2016].

Coker, Joanna, "How to reduce impact of divorce on children". (London: oneplusone, 2014). Available at: **http://www.oneplusone.org.uk/blog/joanna-coker-how-to-reduce-impact-of-divorce-on-children/** [Accessed 6 February 2016].

Duffy, Lisa, "7 ways Parish Leaders Can Better Serve Divorced Catholics". (1 August 2015) Available at: **http://www.catholicmatch.com/institute/2015/08/5-ways-parish-leaders-can-better-serve-divorced-catholics/** [Accessed 6 February 2016].

divorcedcatholic.com [website run by Vince Frese] Available at **http://divorcedcatholic.com/** [Accessed 6 February 2016].

Evangelical Presbyterian Churches, "Divorce and Remarriage" (Livonia, MI: Evangelical Presbyterian Churches: 1995). Available at: **http://www.epc.org/positionpapers** [Accessed 6 February 2016].

Goodstein, Laurie and Povoledo, Elisabeta, "Amid Splits, Catholic Bishops Crack Open Door on Divorce" *New York Times* (24 October 2015). Available at: **http://www.nytimes.com/2015/10/25/world/europe/synod-makes-overture-to-the-divorced-but-rejects-gay-marriage.html?_r=0** [Accessed 6 February 2016].

Message of the XI Ordinary General Assembly of the Synod of Bishops. (Rome: Vatican, 2005) Available at: **http://www.vatican.va/roman_curia/synod/documents/rc_s ynod_doc_20051022_message-synod_en.html** [Accessed 6 February 2016].

Oneplusone: Strengthening relationships (London: 2016) Available at: **http://www.oneplusone.org.uk/** [Accessed 6 February 2016].

Religious Tolerance, "The range of religious views on divorce and remarriage". Ontario: Religious Tolerance, 2015. Available at: **http://www.religioustolerance.org/chr_divo.htm** [Accessed 6 February 2016].

Scalia, Elizabeth, "Pope Francis's quiet campaign to rethink divorce in the Catholic Church" *The Guardian* (5 February 2014). Available at: **http://www.theguardian.com/commentisfree/2014/feb/05/pope-francis-catholic-church-divorce-change** [Accessed 6 February 2016].

The Canons and Decrees of the Sacred and Oecumenical Council of Trent in J. Waterworth (Trans. and Ed), (London: Dolman, 1848) [originally in Latin in 1563). Available at: **http://history.hanover.edu/texts/trent.html** [Accessed 6 February 2016].

The Christian Institute, "Marriage and the Family" (Newcastle Upon Tyne, 2016). Available at: **http://www.christian.org.uk/resources/theology/apologetics/marriage-and-family/divorce/** [Accessed 6 February 2016].

The Church of England Divorce (2016) Available at: **https://www.churchofengland.org/our-views/marriage,-family-and-sexuality-issues/divorce.aspx** [Accessed 6 February 2016].

The Westminster Confession of Faith (1647) Available at: **http://www.reformed.org/documents/wcf_with_proofs/** [Accessed 6 February 2016].

Van Biema, David, "An Evangelical Rethink on Divorce?" *TIME* (15 November 2007), p. 1. Available at: **http://content.time.com/time/nation/article/0,8599,1680709, 00.html** [Accessed 6 February 2016].

Secondary Literature (Academic)

Adams, Jay E., Marriage, Divorce and Remarriage in the Bible: A Fresh Look at What Scripture Teaches. (Grand Rapids, MI: Zondervan, 1980).

Amato, Paul R., "The consequences of divorce for adults and children," *Journal of Marriage and Family* Vol. 62, No. 4 (2000), pp. 1269-1287.

Amato, Paul R. "Research on Divorce: Continuing Trends and New Developments," *Journal of Marriage and Family* Vol. 72, No. 3, (2010) pp. 650-666.

Amato, Paul R., Booth, Alan, Johnson, David R. and Rogers, Stacy J., *Alone Together: How Marriage in America is Changing.* (Cambridge, MA: Harvard University Press, 2007).

Amato, Paul R. and Keith, Bruce. "Parental Divorce and the Well-Being of Children: A Meta-Analysis," *Psychological Bulletin* Vol. 110, No. 1 (1991), pp. 26-46.

Balswick, Jack O. and Balswick, Judith K., *The Family: A Christian Perspective on the Contemporary Home.* Third edition. (Grand Rapids, MI: Baker Academic, 2007).

Blomquist, Jean M. "The effect of the divorce experience on spiritual growth" *Pastoral Psychology* Vol. 34, No. 2, (1985), pp. 82-91.

Braun, Michael A. Second Class Christians? A New Approach to the Dilemma of Divorced Persons in the Church (Downers Grove, IL: InterVarsity Press, 1989).

Chibi, Andrew A., "'Turpidudinem uxoris fratris tui non revelavit': John Stokesly and the Divorce Question" *Sixteenth Century Journal* Vol. 25, No. 2 (1994), pp. 387-397.

Cook, Carol J., "The Practice of Marriage and Family Counseling and Liberal Protestant Christianity" in Jill Duba Onedera (Ed.), *The Role of Religion in Marriage and Family Counseling* (London and New York: Routledge, 2008), pp. 73-88.

Davidson, Graeme, When the Vow Breaks: Contemplating Christian Divorce (London: SPCK, 2009).

Dejong, Peter and Wilson, Donald R., *Husband and Wife: The Sexes in Scripture and Society* (Grand Rapids, MI: Zondervan, 1979).

Demo, David H. and Acock, Alan C. "The Impact of Divorce upon Children," *Journal of Marriage and Family* Vol. 50, No. 3, (2000), pp. 619-648.

Duffy, Lisa and Frese, Vince, *Divorced. Catholic. Now What?* Third edition. (Marietta, CA: Journey of Hope Productions, 2011).

Evans, Craig A., *The Bible Knowledge Background Commentary: Matthew-Luke* (Eastbourne: Kingsway Communications, 2003).

Efird, James M., *Marriage and Divorce: What the Bible Says* (Eugene, OR: Wipf and Stock, 2001).

Fagan, Patrick F. and Churchill, Aaron, *The Effects of Divorce on Children: Research Synthesis.* (Washington, DC: Marriage & Religion Research Institute, 1999).

Fiorenza, Francis Schüssler, "Marriage". In Francis Schüssler Fiorenza (Ed.), *Systematic Theology: Roman Catholic Perspectives.* Second edition. Minneapolis, MN: Fortress Press, pp. 583-620.

Forster, Greg, Healing Love's Wounds: A Pastoral Approach to Divorce and Remarriage (Grand Rapids, MI: Zondervan, 1995).

Forster, Greg, "The Changing Face of Marriage and Divorce" *Anvil* Vol. 17, No. 3, (2000), pp. 167-178.

France, R. T., The Gospel According to Matthew: An Introduction and Commentary (Leicester: InterVarsity Press, 1985).

Garland, Diana S. Richmond and Garland, David E., *Beyond Companionship: Christians in Marriage* (Eugene, OR: Wipf and Stock, 2003).

Geisler, Norman L., *Christian Ethics: Contemporary Issues and Options.* Second edition. (Grand Rapids, MI: Baker Publishing Group, 2010).

Goddard, Andrew, "Theology and Practices in the Evangelical Churches" in Adrian Thatcher (Ed.), *The Oxford Handbook of Theology, Sexuality and Gender* (Oxford: Oxford University Press, 2014), pp. 377-394.

Grunlan, Stephen A., *Marriage and the Family: A Christian Perspective.* Revised edition. (Grand Rapids, MI: Zondervan, 1999).

Gundry, Patricia, *Heirs Together* (Grand Rapids: Zondervan, 1980).

Henking, Susan E., "Sociological Christianity and Christian Sociology: The Paradox of Early American Sociology" *Religion and American Culture: A Journal of Interpretation* Vol. 3, No. 1 (1993), pp. 49-67.

Heth, William A., "Jesus on Divorce: How My Mind Has Changed" *The Southern Baptist Journal of Theology* Vol, 6 (2002), pp. 4-29.

Horsley, Richard A., *Abingdon New Testament Commentaries: I Corinthians* (Nashville, TX: Abingdon Press, 1998).

Houck, Don and Houck, LaDean, *The Ex Factor: Dealing with Your Former Spouse* (Grand Rapids, MI: Revell, 1997).

House, H. Wayne, "Introduction" in H. Wayne House (Ed.), *Divorce and Remarriage: Four Christian Views* (Downers Grove, IL: InterVarsity Press, 1990), pp. 9-11.

Howell, John C, *Equality and Submission in Marriage* (Nashville: Broadman, 1979)

Instone-Brewer, David, *Divorce and Remarriage in the Bible.* (Grand Rapids: Eerdmans, 2002).

Jones, David Clyde, "A Note on the LXX of Malachi 2:16" *Journal of Biblical Literature* Vol. 109, No. 4, (1990), pp. 683-685.

Kalmijn, Matthijs, "Country Differences in the Effects of Divorce on Well-Being: the Role of Norms, Support, and Selectivity" *European Sociological Review* vol. 26, no. 4 (2010), pp. 475-490.

Kreeft, Peter, *Making Sense out of Suffering* (Ann Arbor: Servant Books, 1986).

Laney, J. Carl, "No Divorce and No Remarriage" in H. Wayne House (Ed.), *Divorce and Remarriage: Four Christian Views* (Downers Grove, IL: InterVarsity Press, 1990), pp. 15-54.

Lawlor, Michael, *Marriage and the Catholic Church: Disputed Questions* (Collegeville, MN: Liturgical Press, 2002).

MacRae, James A. Jr., "The Secularization of Divorce", in Beverly Duncan and Otis Dudly Duncan (Eds.), *Sex Typing and Social Roles* (New York: Academic Press, 1978), pp. 227 – 242.

Moxnes, Halvor, "What is family? Problems in constructing early Christian families. In Halvor Moxnes, (Ed.), *Constructing Early Christian Families: Family as Social Reality and Metaphor* (London: Psychology Press, 1997), pp. 13-41.

New Advent, "Divorce (in Moral Theology)", in *The Catholic Encyclopedia* (2015). Available at: **http://www.newadvent.org/cathen/05054c.htm** [Accessed 2 October 2015].

Onedera, Jill D., "The Practice of Marriage and Family Counseling and Catholicism" in Jill Duba Onedera (Ed.), *The Role of Religion in Marriage and Family Counseling* (London and New York: Routledge, 2008), pp. 37-54.

Parmenter, Bruce, Christians Caught in the Divorce Trap: Helping Families Recover from Divorce (Joplin, MO: College Press Publishing Company).

Phillips, Roderick, *Untying the Knot: A Short History of Divorce* (Cambridge: Cambridge University Press, 1991).

Quinn, Kathy S., "The Worst Rejection" (2016). Available at: **http://whosoever.org/v5i2/quinn.html** [Accessed 6 February 2016].

Root, Andrew, The Children of Divorce: The Loss of Family as the Loss of Being (Grand Rapids, MI: Baker Academic, 2010).

Segal, Robert A., "In Defense of the Comparative Method" *Numen* Vol. 48, No. 3, pp. 339-373.

Snuth, David L., "Divorce and Remarriage from the Early Church to John Wesley" *Trinity Journal* Vol. 11, No. 2 (1990), pp. 131-142.

Stein, Robert H., "Is it lawful for a man to divorce his wife?" *Journal of the Evangelical Theological Society* Vol. 22, No. 2, pp. 115-121.

Stott, John, Our Social and Sexual Revolution: Major Issues for a New Century (Grand Rapids: Baker, 1999).

Teachman, Jay D. and Paasch, Kathleen M., *The Future of Children* Vol. 4, No. 1 (1994), pp. 63-83.

Thatcher, Adrian, Marriage after Modernity: Christian Marriage in Postmodern Times (New York: New York University Press, 1999).

Thatcher, Adrian, *Living Together and Christian Ethics* (Cambridge: Cambridge University Press, 2002).

Thomas, Curtis C., Practical Wisdom for Pastors: Words of Encouragement and Counsel for a Lifetime of Ministry (Wheaton, IL: Crossway, 2001).

Thornton, Arland., "Changing Attitudes toward Separation and Divorce: Causes and Consequences" *American Journal of Sociology* Vol. 90, No. 4, (1985), pp. 856-872.

Wenham, Gordon J. and Heth, William E., *Jesus and Divorce: Towards an Evangelical Understanding of New Testament Teaching*. Second edition. (Carlisle: Paternoster, 1997).

Weitzman, Lenore, *The Divorce Revolution* (New York: Free Press, 1985).

Wiesner-Hanks, Merry, Christianity and Sexuality in the Early Modern World: Regulating Desire, Reforming Practice. Second edition. (Abingdon: Routledge, 2010).

Wilcox, W. Bradford, *Soft Patriarchs, New Men: How Christianity Shapes Fathers and Husbands* (Chicago and London: University of Chicago Press, 2004).

Witte, John Jr. and Kingdon, Robert M., *Sex, Marriage and Family in John Calvin's Geneva* (Grand Rapids, MI: Eerdmans, 2005).

Zink, Daniel W., "The Practice of Marriage and Family Counseling and Conservative Christianity". In Jill Duba Onedera (Ed.), *The Role of Religion in Marriage and Family Counseling* (London and New York: Routledge, 2008), pp. 55-72.

Printed in Great Britain
by Amazon

30766485R00066